The
Far
Side
of
the
Sea

2003-2004 NMI
MISSION EDUCATION RESOURCES

❊ ❊ ❊

READING BOOKS

THE FAR SIDE OF THE SEA
From the Philippines to Ukraine
by Lynn DiDominicis

FLOODS OF COMPASSION*
Hope for Honduras
by Paul Jetter

IMPACT!*
Work and Witness Miracles
by J. Wesley Eby

THE JAGGED EDGE OF SOMEWHERE*
by Amy Crofford

THE LAND OF THE LONG WHITE CLOUD
Nazarenes in New Zealand
by Connie Griffith Patrick

SECOND WIND
Running the Race in Retirement
by Sherry Pinson

*Youth Books

❊ ❊ ❊

ADULT MISSION EDUCATION RESOURCE BOOK

CALLED TO GO
Edited by Wes Eby

The Far Side of the Sea

From the Philippines to Ukraine

by
Lynn DiDominicis

Nazarene Publishing House
Kansas City, Missouri

Copyright 2003
by Nazarene Publishing House

ISBN 083-412-0186

Printed in the United States of America

Editor: Wes Eby
Cover Design: Michael Walsh

10 9 8 7 6 5 4 3 2 1

Dedication

To my parents, Paul and Marion Peterson,
and Chicago First Church of the Nazarene,
for giving me a great and godly heritage.

Contents

"If I settle on *the far side of the sea*,

even there your hand will guide me,

your right hand will hold me fast"

(Psalm 139:9*b*-10, italics added).

Lynn DiDominicis is a teacher, writer, and workshop presenter along with being a busy wife, mother, and grandmother.

A third-generation Nazarene, she is active in her church, Fairview Village, in the greater Philadelphia area. She has served as the local Nazarene Missions International (NMI) president and is still a member of the NMI council.

Lynn has been a member of the Adult Mission Education (AME) committee for eight years and has written several of the AME lessons. She has also contributed to the Children's Mission Education (CME) committee as a writer and resource for the lessons.

An educator by training, she is currently employed at Penn View Christian School, where she teaches family and consumer science to seventh and eighth graders and language arts to sixth graders.

Lynn lives in Trappe, Pennsylvania, with her husband, Denny.

Foreword

On a late summer Wednesday evening more than 15 years ago, Bob and Colleen Skinner attended Bible study at the Overland Park, Kansas, Church of the Nazarene where I served as pastor. They still had Idaho dust on their shoes and unpacked boxes in tow, having just arrived in the city days before bent on attending Nazarene Theological Seminary (NTS). At the close of the service, I invited the Skinners to join me in my study for conversation. Sixty minutes later, they left with an invitation to serve the church as children's pastors. And serve they did for the duration of their time in Kansas City.

In the intervening years, our paths have crossed more frequently than I ever dreamed possible when they left Kansas City to assume their first missionary career assignment to the Philippines. The Skinners happened to be in our home when they learned they had been reassigned after just one term in the Asia-Pacific Region to somewhere in the former Soviet Union. Their story has been a living testimony to simple faith, deep trust, and dogged determination to "seek first the Kingdom."

Colleen, on whom the accent falls in this book, is absolutely key to the Skinner equation. Though she would be the first to object to any inflated appraisal of her work and is self-effacing to a fault, she consistently exhibits the constancy of grace. In seasons of blessings and in the hour of adversity, Colleen bears a resilient smile and exudes confidence that God is God and that's sufficient for her.

I have eaten with the Skinners in their compact apartment in Kyiv, Ukraine. I have joined them in song and sacrament at a country dacha not far from Moscow. I have watched them minister to strangers while home on furlough. I have witnessed them turning aside gifts for themselves, insisting that someone on the mission field needed it more than they. I have watched them corral three lively boys. I have kept company with them at general assemblies and retreated with them in the hills of Tennessee. In all those times and places, their commitment to Christ and the church has been unswerving.

All of that is not an attempt to deify the Skinners; it is to say they lovingly reflect the grace of God. Their winsome smiles, genuine warmth, and authentic expression are refreshing. To know them is to love them.

Randall E. Davey
Pastor, Seattle Aurora Church of the Nazarene,
Shoreline, Washington

Introduction

Colleen Skinner was a missionary kid (MK) by chance. Then God called, and she became a missionary by choice. Today she and her husband, Bob, are career missionaries, serving in Ukraine with their three sons—Robby, Michael, and Joshua.

Colleen received her legacy from her parents, Ronald and Neva Beech, who were Nazarene missionaries for 31 years.

During Colleen's years at Northwest Nazarene College (now University), the Lord gave her a special scripture: "If I settle on *the far side of the sea*, even there your hand will guide me, your right hand will hold me fast" (Ps. 139:9*b*-10, italics added). This Bible verse has been a stabilizer for more than two decades.

Though Colleen is still young, at least by my standards, this unique lady has lived an extraordinary life. Her travels and experiences, her joys and sorrows, provide authentic examples of God's leading and protection.

I could not have been written this book without Colleen's willingness to give me precious time to tell her story through delightful conversation and sensitive writing. A caring person, she exudes warmth. She made my limited moments with her memorable ones, and I gained great respect for this wonderful individual. In fact, getting to know Colleen and Bob has given me an enhanced appreciation for all our missionaries who sacrifice so much to obey God's call and represent our church on the mission field.

The facts in this book are true. While I have attempted to faithfully record the words of Colleen as she gave them to me, at times I have added to the conversation to make the story more readable and alive.

The Church of the Nazarene has a great mission history and heritage. As we look to the future, we can look back to the people, such as Colleen and Bob, who have settled on *the far side of the sea*, blazing uncharted trails, exploring new paths, gaining fresh insights. Their example challenges all of us to nobler, far-reaching exploits for the Kingdom.

Colleen and Bob Skinner with their sons:
(l. to r.) Michael, Joshua, and Robby.

1
The Legacy Begins

Restless, impatient, Colleen Skinner sat between her mother and father at the Intermountain District Assembly in Idaho. Her third child was due soon. Bob, her husband, was thousands of miles away in Switzerland engaged in church work.

"I didn't feel like an in-charge mother and missionary's wife," Colleen says. "I felt more like the little girl I used to be, sitting comfortably with my parents."

The feeling lingered into the next days as Colleen and the family made plans to celebrate her mom's birthday. But the anticipated celebration also carried a feeling of melancholy, as Mom Beech had been diagnosed with cancer.

"No need for serious concern," the doctor assured the family. "I believe the cancer is treatable."

Party preparations continued. Colleen was pleased to be near her mother for this birthday, especially since the coming of her child was imminent. The birthday was a joyous, festive event; happiness abounded.

Suddenly, Colleen started experiencing labor pains—two weeks early and Bob was still away to boot. All previous birth arrangements were scrapped,

15

and Grandmother Neva was present at the nativity of her newest grandson, Joshua, on May 24, 1997. He was a special baby to her, born just two days after her own birthday. She doted on this wee infant, tenderly caring for him while the new mother rested.

No one could have foreseen that just two weeks later Neva herself would be bedridden, felled by the insidious cancer that attacked with its ugly force. In the following days, Joshua lay on his grandmother's bed, soaking in her attention. She sang soft lullabies to him. She whispered messages of love in his ear. She watched him grow.

A few months later, Neva Beech slipped away from her family, making her journey home to be with Jesus.

As the family gathered for the funeral, Colleen reflected on her parent's lives. Memories—precious memories—flooded her mind and heart.

❋   ❋   ❋

Neva Templeman was raised in a wheat farmer's home on the chilly, windswept plains of northern North Dakota near Minot. Farm life, busy and rugged, helped prepare Neva for the life God had designed for her. With three older half brothers and a younger brother and sister, Neva grew up in a home that required many responsibilities and chores along with numerous give-and-take moments.

Neva's parents were strong Christians and committed Nazarenes. The whole family attended church, which became as natural and routine as breathing. The Lord used this godly parental influence, calling three of the boys to the ministry and one sister to share a parsonage with her pastor-husband.

When Neva took piano lessons, her God-given ability for music became obvious. She often played for her home church, as accomplished musicians seemed to be rare in those days. Her love of music was lifelong.

Colleen's father, Ronald Beech, was born in Victoria, British Columbia, to a Christian family. They moved to Seattle when Ron was two years old. During his growing up years, his parents provided a sound religious heritage for their four children through Methodist and Presbyterian churches. When Ron was a young teenager, his mother and two sisters joined the Church of the Nazarene; however, several years would pass before Ron became a Nazarene too. (Today all four of the Beech children are Nazarenes.)

After high school, Ron served a two-year hitch in the United States Navy. His overseas travels took him across the Pacific Ocean to the Far East, including a few months stay in the Philippines.

Returning home, he entered a private college in Yakima, Washington. While there as a 20-year-old, he joined the Church of the Nazarene, primarily due to the influence of his mother and sisters. This important decision would impact his life in a way that he could not imagine.

Ron took a break from school for a couple of years to work. But in the back of his mind there lingered recurring thoughts of the missionaries he had heard in his younger years. He remembered the missionaries who spoke in church when he was a teen. Back then he told God he would be open to His call, and the months in the Philippines only added to this desire.

Enrolling in Northwest Nazarene College in 1950, he declared education his major. There he met Neva Templeman from North Dakota. Their common interest in Christian service and music brought them together. They joined the Christian Worker's Band and often traveled together to small churches. Ron led the singing; Neva played the piano. This interest led to a mutual attraction . . . courtship . . . engagement . . . marriage. He was a senior; she, a sophomore.

With college diploma in hand, Ron and his bride headed to Kansas City. After one year at Nazarene Theological School (NTS), Ron accepted a position in the public schools, where he taught elementary classes for three years. While in Kansas City, Ron and Neva, under the prompting of the Holy Spirit, applied for mission service. A missionary told them that God could only work if they took the step to file the application. So they did.

Moving back to the Pacific Northwest in 1958 to take a pastorate, Ron and Neva waited patiently, yet they were hopeful the Lord would soon open the door to the mission field. Job and family consumed their lives. Their first child, a daughter, was born in Kansas City, and during the next few years Ron and Neva welcomed four more children into their home, three girls and a boy.

At long last the Beeches were appointed to the Philippines. They left in December 1962 a few weeks after their youngest child was born.

✳ ✳ ✳

As Colleen's mind took a backward flight, she rejoiced in the legacy received from her mother and father. *I'm amazed,* she thought, *that my folks would board a ship for a three-week voyage with five young*

Colleen celebrating her second birthday

children, ranging in age from eight years to four months. They left their home, their families, all that was familiar. And it was right at the Christmas season too! In fact, the Beech family celebrated Christmas and New Year's on that oceangoing vessel. Nothing could distract or deter them from following God's call on their lives.

Colleen knew that her father and mother had encountered many challenges during their first five-year term. Besides the obvious ones of language acquisition and cultural adaptation, they quickly learned that destructive typhoons and floods were ongoing threats. Tropical diseases they had never dealt with before, such as malaria and dengue fever, cropped up. And raising five small children in a community where open sewers were commonplace sometimes tested their commitment.

> I went outside, crawled into one of the big crates where Daddy had been working, and just sobbed.

Soon after arriving in Manila, Colleen's father became quite ill, requiring hospitalization. He clung to life in desperate need of a blood transfusion, but no Filipino could be found with his rare blood type. Mom Beech did not tell her children how serious their dad's illness was. *But I just knew,* Colleen thought. *Somehow I knew that my daddy was very, very sick.*

The family's crates had just cleared customs not long before, and the Beeches were finally unpacking and getting settled when he became sick. *I was so devastated,* Colleen remembered, *that I went outside, crawled into one of the big crates where Daddy had been working, and just sobbed. I cried out to my Heavenly Father to somehow spare him. And God did! Two American women from a United States Air Force base donated the blood that saved his life.*

Although only four years old, Colleen learned a lesson from that dark valley that would carry her through other dark valleys throughout her life. The faith, courage, and perseverance her mother and father lived before their family, even in difficult times, served as a constant example and testimony of God's great grace and loving care for His children. It was a solid heritage.

Music continually rang through the Beech home. While Ron strummed the guitar, Neva played the piano, organ, or accordion. From the time of their college days, they sang together. As the five children grew up, they added more harmony to their parents' duets. During frequent power outages in the Philippines, Mom Beech sat at the piano, often in complete darkness, and sang, encouraging all the family to join in. And since Filipinos love music, rarely a Sunday passed when the family did not share some songs in the worship services. Neva made sure her children were always ready with a song.

One amusing incident stood out in Colleen's memories of those early years. Her grandparents and a great-aunt on her mother's side were visiting the Beech family during their first term in Manila. The Filipino pastor wanted to honor the guests from the United States, so he decided to preach in English the first Sunday they were there. "How did you enjoy the message?" Neva asked. "Enjoy? I didn't under-stand a word he said," her mother laughed, thinking the question was a joke. The English-speaking visi-tors had no clue the sermon was in their native tongue. *No one got much from that poor pastor's mes-sage that day,* Colleen remembered with a smile.

Over the years, Colleen's brother, Barry, provid-ed lots of amusement and laughter to his family. What an imitator he was! He could ape just about anything and kept everyone entertained.

While the Beeches taught at the Bible college, they ate supper earlier than the Filipino kids. Barry's friends were still outside playing when he was called inside to eat. Whenever the lad resisted, he didn't get any supper—or so his parents thought. Actually he was going home with his playmates and eating with them, which had an unexpected side effect. Barry be-gan to eat and like Filipino food better than the meals his mother was preparing. It was a big surprise to his parents when Barry learned the Tagalog language and Filipino customs—especially relishing the food. To this day, he prefers Filipino fare to anything else.

Each furlough year was spent in a different state so the Beeches could live near their parents and take advantage of the limited time at home. All five chil-dren often stayed with their grandparents, especially if school schedules did not allow the kids to travel with their parents on deputation. *I'm deeply grateful for my godly grandparents, who loved and supported our family and God's call on our lives,* Colleen thought, her eyes becoming moist. *Although times with my grandparents were few and far between, they were always greatly anticipated. My memories of them are keen and deeply treasured.*

✻ ✻ ✻

As Colleen pondered her childhood days, she thought about the church her parents planted, starting with a handful of people meeting each week in their home for singing, prayer, Bible study, and fellowship. *We kids had the special privilege of being more than observers. We were drawn right into the middle of*

Colleen, homecoming queen at Faith Academy
in the Philippines, 1977

it. I can still feel the excitement of the day our family moved into a house next to the empty lot where the new church would be built. How thrilling to watch the daily progress and to be right there at the center of all the activity. When the building was completed, we, too, were part of the teams that went out to invite families to Sunday School and church. And this is the church where at age seven I gave my heart to Jesus Christ.

Over the years, the Lord has blessed those early seeds planted in love and obedience, for now that church is the largest Nazarene congregation in the Philippines. Pastored by a gifted Filipino, he was one of the first young teens to come to the church when the Beeches ministered there many years ago.

❋ ❋ ❋

In the midst of her reflection, Colleen lingered over one very "precious memory." During her parents' first furlough in 1967, she—an eight-year-old, soon-to-be third grader—attended a girl's summer camp where her mother was the missionary speaker.

During that week, I heard Mom share her missionary call, she remembered. *For the first time I clearly realized exactly what my parents were doing in the Philippines. Up until that time, these islands had just been home to me. I had not understood that they had traveled halfway around the*

> I heard God's voice that night, clearly, distinctly. And from that time on, the Lord confirmed and strengthened His call on my life—even to go to "the far side of the sea."

24

world because of a call from God, that they were in the Far East because they loved the Lord and desired to obey Him.

One evening following the service, the camp counselor asked if any of the girls in their cabin felt the Lord speaking to them about being a missionary. Colleen raised her hand. *I heard God's voice that night, clearly, distinctly. And from that time on, the Lord confirmed and strengthened His call on my life— even to go to "the far side of the sea."*

❄ ❄ ❄

During the funeral Colleen looked around at her four siblings and their mates—her older sister, Barbara, a teacher, and rancher husband, Mark York . . . the sister just younger than she, Cathy, a speech ther-

Beech family reunion in 1994

25

apist, and attorney Kevin Borger . . . the youngest sister, Lynette, a paralegal, and Dan Cochran, an educator . . . her only brother, Barry, a purchasing manager for a power company, and Molly, a sister of missionary Verne Ward Jr.

Colleen bubbled with pride and love for each of them. The five Beech kids had grown up together in the Philippines. The quintet had shared happy, carefree moments along with the three Ts—trials, testings, and troubles. And now these MKs are all Christians and active in the Church of the Nazarene. This knowledge helped to ease her sorrow and pain as she and the others said good-bye to their dear mother.

Then Colleen glanced at her father.* She knew he was grieving, and his loneliness would be great. He and Neva had lived more than 43 years *together.* They had served in the Philippines for 31 years *together.* After retirement they had returned to the Philippines *together* three times for short assignments. And they had been Nazarenes in Volunteer Service (NIVS) *together* for one year in Samoa. Their entire lives since college had been marked by *togetherness.* Colleen thought, *What a heritage I have! What a marvelous legacy!*

---

*Ron Beech married Doris Cook, a widow, in September 2001.

2
Love Story

Finally, college! Though leaving her family in the Philippines was difficult, Colleen anticipated campus life at Northwest Nazarene College (NNC) with lots of other young people. The settling-in time was brief and easy.

With her inherited love of music and singing, the college choir beckoned irresistibly, and Colleen signed up. Now one would think that she would be content to stay at the college and absorb life in the United States. But not this MK.

"The choir had a strong missions emphasis," Colleen says, "and our concert tours meant travel, lots of it. For four summers I sang with the choir on different mission fields." South Africa, Swaziland, Zimbabwe, Papua New Guinea, Spain, Portugal, Denmark, Australia, and New Zealand were included in the group's itineraries—each country so different from the Philippines.

"Each summer we were stretched in a new and different culture," Colleen says. "And in each country we visited I found myself on my knees, saying, 'Oh yes, Lord. I'm willing to come back here if this is where You want me to serve You.'

"By the time I finished my degree at NNC, I felt I could honestly say with all my heart, 'Lord, I will go anywhere—absolutely *anywhere*—You can use me." But never in her wildest dreams did she think His call would take her to what had seemed to be the scariest place in the world, the Soviet Union.

"Once again," she says, "God has proven to me there is no place on earth that His grace has not gone before and that 'if I settle on the far side of the sea, even there [His] hand will guide me, [His] right hand will hold me fast.'"

Colleen graduated from college unattached and with no spouse in the future. She had had one this-could-lead-to-marriage friendship with a fellow student and choir member. Although this young man and Colleen had shared in all the same mission opportunities, their inner experiences and God's specific direction were not the same. "In the weeks lead-

Colleen graduating from college, 1982

ing up to graduation," Colleen admits, "I had to deal with the issue of being completely obedient to God's call and not compromising, even if it meant giving up an enjoyable and close relationship."

What a difficult choice for a young person! But Colleen came to the point that she was willing to be a missionary even if it meant going alone, knowing that God would never forsake her. "Sadly, I broke off the relationship," she says. "Obeying God was more important to me than finding a husband."

With college behind her, Colleen began working in the public school system in Nampa, Idaho, with migrant children, teaching English as a second language. This was yet another cross-cultural experience that God used to help stretch and equip her.

Then, unexpectedly, the pastor at Nampa College Church invited her to join the staff as an assistant to the youth pastor. This created a problem. She was member of First Nazarene in the same city, deeply involved and loving it. "I hated the thought of uprooting," Colleen says, "even though I know this is a missionary's lifestyle. After praying and wrestling with this decision, I felt God swing open a new door for me." Little did she know what lay ahead.

About that time another nearby church in Meridian was looking for a youth pastor. This church had scheduled a weekend youth retreat with a recent graduate of Boise State University as the speaker. The planners invited Colleen to come and lead the music. What she didn't know was the scheming going on behind her back. In preparing for the retreat, the leaders assigned the participants designated seats, and

Colleen's name tag was strategically placed beside the guest worker, Bob Skinner.

❋ ❋ ❋

Robert William Skinner II, known by most people as Bob, is the second child of Bill and Nancy. He and his three sisters—Phyllis Ann Vermillyea, Susan Barbara Tavernier, and Carol Marie Skinner—grew up in Canyon City, a tiny community in eastern Oregon.

> **Bob had been skunked once more—this time by a huge, lumbering, shaggy-haired beast.**

"Bob was a happy, normal child," his mother says, "and he just loved to tease his sisters." One of his special childhood memories is spending summers with his maternal grandmother on the upper peninsula in Michigan. Their cabin home was nestled by a private lake, with a forest of birch trees and verdant ferns. This was a kid's dream—lots of territory to explore, animals to chase, and water to swim in.

One hot summer day, 12-year-old Bob and his cousin Steve took their BB guns to hunt skunks in an abandoned dump. All the male cousins had stinky skunk hides, trophies of their shooting skills, drying in the garage. Except Bob. You might say he had been skunked in killing skunks! This day was his last try before returning home. Suddenly, Steve gave a bloodcurdling scream. All Bob could do was take a quick glance as he raced Steve down the road. When they arrived at the cabin, the boys' story seemed so incredulous that everyone piled in a jeep and headed

30

for the dump. But the evidence was unmistakable. A bear really had been there. But, alas, Bob had been skunked once more—this time by a huge, lumbering, shaggy-haired beast.

At an early age Bob began to display confidence. As a six-year-old he announced to the congregation after singing with a group, "We sounded good." Later as an older teen, he went elk hunting with his dad. After dark the two became separated and Bob was confused as to the location of their pickup. As a result he spent the night in the woods alone. "But he really used his head," his mother remembers. "He walked around and around because he knew if lay down he would become hypothermic. At daylight he walked out of the forest safe and sound—though a bit frosty—to where his father and I waited anxiously at the truck."

Bob's family were churchgoing folks; however, they did not have a personal relationship with Christ. In 1971 both Bill and Nancy became born-again Christians, and she was baptized. Two years later, Bob accepted the Lord at a community youth Bible study. In 1975 he and his father were baptized by Pastor Herb Cummings of the John Day Church of the Nazarene.

Tall, broad-shouldered, and muscular, Bob landed a football scholarship at Boise State University (BSU) in Idaho as a defensive lineman. He even considered a career in professional football.

During his junior year at BSU, Bob became involved with Campus Crusade for Christ. He spent one summer in New Jersey at the seashore involved in beach and town ministries. This experience served as a catalyst to turn him on to the Lord. He became a bold witness for Christ, which included evangelizing his teammates in Athletes in Action.

One day the Holy Spirit used the Word to speak to Bob's willing heart: "How, then, can they call on the one they have not believed in? And how can they believe in the one of whom they have not heard? And how can they hear without someone preaching to them? And how can they preach unless they are sent? As it is written, 'How beautiful are the feet of those who bring good news!'" (Rom. 10:14-15). After this encounter with the Lord, Bob made a serious commitment to serve the Lord—wherever that may be. Dreams of professional football evaporated. Instead he accepted a youth pastorate.

✳ ✳ ✳

During the retreat, the schemers watched Bob and Colleen constantly to see if there might be any sparks of interest. At the conclusion, the plotters arranged for Bob to drive Colleen back to town in the director's car instead of riding on the youth bus. This matchmaking game continued throughout the summer, making it difficult for a normal, natural friendship to develop. "I reached the point of wanting to avoid Bob altogether," Colleen admits. "Finally in September Bob pleaded with the main instigator to please back off."

> **Finally Bob pleaded with the main instigator to please back off.**

Since both Bob and Colleen were working full-time with teens, they found themselves involved in many of the same activities and often at the same functions. The more they were together, the greater the attraction.

Their first "real" date took place at a Mexican restaurant. (This is still their favorite food, but none can be found in Ukraine.) Between enchiladas and tacos, they talked . . . and talked . . . and talked. Chips and salsa devoured, they talked on and on and on. Finally someone from the kitchen approached them and kindly asked them to leave, as it was past closing time. Looking around, they saw the chairs had been turned upside down on the tables, and they were the only customers left.

Rushing to the cash register, apologizing profusely, they were prepared to pay and hustle out the door. Another surprise. Someone had already paid the bill. This anonymous benefactor remains unknown. "We still smile every time we think of that first date," Colleen says. "The funny thing is that even in married life we have become so engrossed in conversation we've been asked to leave places. And there's always more to talk about."

Colleen made an important, even amazing, discovery about Bob during their courtship. After his junior year during a summer missions project, he felt God's leading toward missions. He wanted to obtain some practical experience in a church and then attend Nazarene Theological Seminary (NTS) for formal training. "That was the same exact path I felt God leading me," Colleen says. "I had already re-

Colleen and Bob's wedding, 1985

ceived information from NTS and World Mission. Over and over the Lord confirmed that He was directing us to serve Him in ministry."

The next year Bob proposed, and Colleen didn't hesitate to say yes. The wedding was planned for the following year when her parents would be in the States for furlough. Bob and Colleen said their "I dos" on May 31, 1985, at College Church in Nampa. "It was a wonderful, *wonderful* celebration of love and God's clear leading in our lives," Colleen says.

For the next year they worked together in Bob's church in Meridian before the Lord led them to Asia-Pacific Nazarene Theological Seminary in

Manila. They were the only American students among Filipinos, Chinese, Koreans, East Indians, Indonesian, and Africans. "We had the rich experience of living on campus among these diverse cultures and people," Colleen says. "Our education here extended far beyond the classroom and textbooks."

In 1987 Bob and Colleen transferred to NTS in Kansas City, where they both finished their master's degrees. During this time Bob served as children's and visitation pastor at the Overland Park church. Their engaging personalities, Colgate smiles, and teddy-bear hugs, along with God-endowed gifts and graces, endeared this handsome couple to their congregation and impacted the lives of the children for eternity. Here Colleen gave birth to Robby, their first son, a towheaded tyke that captivated everyone.

When the Skinners completed their education, the church appointed them as career missionaries to the Philippines in 1990. Colleen was returning home once more. "What more could I ever hope for?" she says. "Back to the place of my childhood. Back to the only home I really knew until college. Back to the country where Bob and I attended school for a year. Yes, this was *home*."

3
Back to the Philippines

The Skinners drove southward from Manila, dodging and weaving through brightly decorated jeepneys, tricycles (motorized bicycles with side-cars), trucks, autos, carts, animals, and pedestrians. Each one claimed the right-of-way, creating a traffic challenge—indeed, a hazard. A normal three-hour drive often took five or six instead.

Bob and Colleen's destination was Batangas, a port city that would be their base of operation. Assigned to the Luzon Council, they would be involved in evangelizing and church planting as well as assisting established churches.

This assignment required them to travel, at times, by boat to neighboring islands to visit Nazarene congregations. "Some of our most memorable times as a family were spent going to these fervent, young churches," Colleen says. "Often we accompanied medical, evangelism, or Work and Witness teams. Each time we returned home we were exhausted in body, yet strengthened and encouraged in spirit. We could see God's hand so plainly at work in these eager, growing Christians."

One island, the location of a large Nazarene church, had no electricity, no running water, no

Bob and Colleen ready for a jeepney ride

medical facility, and no means of motor transportation. The only way to leave Isle Verde was by a wooden boat with bamboo outriggers that left once a day at 3:30 A.M. "Health problems and emergencies were the source of great concern," Colleen says. "Families often lost a child in birth because C-sections and other common medical practices were not available. As a result, the people resorted to witch doctors and pagan rituals out of fear and superstition."

Tucked away in Colleen's indelible memories are the times spent on this island. Rising at two o'clock in the morning, they would crawl from under mosquito nets, quietly gather their belongings in the dim flickering light of a rag wick soaked in a jar of kerosene, and scoop up slumbering little ones. Cautiously descending the creaking bamboo steps of the pastor's little palm house, they would walk single file on the dirt path down the mountain to the outrigger boat waiting below. Often torrents of rain turned the trail into thick mud, making the trek even more arduous in the darkness.

> They hugged their dear brothers and sisters good-bye, piled on the boat with all the other travelers—along with pigs, goats, chickens, and sacks of produce—and sailed out into the shadowy sea.

"The little torches we carried were crucial to knowing where to take the next step," Colleen remembers. "Invariably, someone in our little caravan would begin to sing softly. 'Thy word is a lamp unto my feet, and a light unto my path' or 'Send the light, the blessed gospel light. \ Let it shine from shore to shore.' In hushed tones we'd all join in, gaining both outward and inward strength."

Once on the shore, they hugged their dear brothers and sisters good-bye, piled on the boat with all the other travelers—along with pigs, goats, chickens, and sacks of produce—and sailed out into the shadowy sea. Looking back at the island, all they could really make out were tiny, twinkling lights sparsely scattered across the great looming silhouette of the mountain.

"Without fail," Colleen says, "my heart would flood with overwhelming gratitude at the unending mercies of God. In the depths of a darkness far greater than that of the night, the pure light of Jesus

Christ was blazing brightly on the top of that mountain in the form of a Church of the Nazarene. There, true peace, joy, and hope were being proclaimed loudly and clearly."

* * *

Smoky Mountain. Just the mention of the name evokes negative thoughts and emotions to anyone who has ever visited there. Located in metropolitan Manila, Smoky Mountain is a seven-story high mound of garbage, the main dumping ground for a city of more than 10 million people. The garbage constantly smolders, causing an ever-present haze over that part of the city. Accompanying the smoke is an overpowering stench that lingers in the nostrils.

Over many years, due to the shortage of land, housing, and jobs, hundreds of people have moved to

Smoky Mountain

Smoky Mountain, making it their home. Building shacks out of whatever materials can be scavenged, the squatters construct their homes and set up house-keeping.

Colleen admits that she was not prepared physically, mentally, or emotionally for her experience with Smoky Mountain when she and Bob participated with a medical and evangelistic team. "All five of my senses were jolted that day," she says, "beginning with the repulsive odor while we were still a long way off."

As Colleen and the others inched along, they tried to sidestep broken glass and rusty tin cans.

As the team drove up on the mound and parked the bus, Colleen felt a surge of hot, burning tears well up as instantly scores of curious children came scurrying to them from every direction. "I was overcome with the thought that those dear little ones actually lived there."

Looking around at the shacks the Filipinos had pieced together, the lump in Colleen's throat grew larger. She noted simple, handmade curtains and tin cans with potted plants or flowers in some of the windows. "Here were touches of beauty in the midst of dire poverty," she says.

As the team members gathered their supplies and equipment from the bus, tiny eager hands, amid laughter and giggling, joined theirs to set up the clinic. "My next unsettling discovery," Colleen says, "was the bouncing sensation when I walked. Each step raised a cloud of dust and stench. As I looked closer, garbage. Tons and tons of garbage."

As Colleen and the others inched along, they tried to sidestep broken glass and rusty tin cans. They noticed that many of the kids were barefooted or only had thinly worn thongs. Some had T-shirts and shorts; a few, completely naked. Nagging flies covered open infected sores on their bodies. *What about sanitation?* she wondered, *and drinking water? What about rats and cockroaches and mosquitoes?*

The group had learned this area of Manila had the highest rate of murder, drug addiction, gambling,

Bob and Colleen with Robby in the Philippines, 1991

and crime of every type. *What difference can we really make in this overwhelming situation?*

Shaded from the scorching sun by a large tarp, the team began singing. As more children gathered, along with families and neighbors, voices joined in scripture choruses and songs of praise to the Good Shepherd, who knows each sheep by name. "Through prayer, picture Bible stories, testimonies, and a brief sermon," Colleen says, "we tried to introduce these dear people to the only One who gives true life and hope."

Then began the long, tedious hours of never-ending lines, both medical and dental, as the team members cared and prayed for each person and his or her special needs. Treatment included hundreds of festering sores, eye/ear/throat infections, and stomach/intestinal problems. Many had their heads com-

Colleen helping prepare a Filipino meal, 1993

42

Bob helping with a Work and Witness team, 1993

pletely shaved for treatment of lice. Even a few minor surgeries and stitches were part of the day's health care, performed right there on folding tables in the open air. "We prayed desperately that no worse infections would set in," Colleen says.

As the long day came to an end, the group had distributed all of their medicines, vitamins, Bibles, and gospel tracts. But one last challenge remained.

"Some of these people had prepared food for us to eat," Colleen remembers. "Eat? After all I had seen and smelled and heard and felt that day? How could I? But we sang and prayed. And then we ate together. And yes, by God's grace, I joined in. I can never forget these precious people. More importantly, God will never forget them."

The evangelistic and medical teams journeyed

to Smoky Mountain with great hope of bringing help and change. But as so often happens, God used the poor—even the humble residents of a huge city dump—to bring changes in the hearts and lives of those who came to minister. "God vividly reminded us," Colleen says, "of the words of Christ: 'Blessed are the poor in spirit: for theirs is the kingdom of heaven. . . . Blessed are they which hunger and thirst after righteousness: for they shall be filled'" (Matt. 5:3, 6, KJV).

4
Doctor, NOW!

"Bob, what's that rash on your face and neck?" Colleen asked, alarm filling her voice.

"I don't know, Co," Bob said. "It just started after I got back from my last island trip. And now it's spreading." Treatment included the usual ointment and salves, but they offered scant relief.

A couple of weeks later, Bob's head starting pounding—a pounding like he had never experienced before. No form of pain medicine relieved the torment. With a complete sense of helplessness, Colleen listened to her husband groaning and wrestling through the long hours. This was followed by a period of high fever and chills, and then the cycle began again.

The Skinners made the long trek to Manila to visit a reputable doctor, who put Bob through extensive lab work. The reports came back with the feared word—*malaria*. Bob had contracted this dreaded disease during the previous weeks of travel. The physician urged Bob to slow down and pace himself. Although highly valuable advice, it provided a challenge for someone so involved in ministry.

This was a difficult time for Colleen. Seeing her big, strapping husband so helpless and in such intense pain, she had to trust God completely for Bob's health and recovery. Through the skill of doc-

Bob *(right)* with members of
Emmanuel Church of the Nazarene

tors and the prayers of dozens, the Lord brought the healing Bob needed.

* * *

Three months later, one of the Bible school students with tuberculosis had to return to her home on the island. Her parents were not Christians, and as so often happens, they blamed their daughter's new religion for causing this misfortune in their lives.

One day Bob sensed an urgency to visit her and encourage the family. But the Skinner's second child was due in two weeks, and they planned to leave for Manila in a couple of days. Colleen and Bob certainly didn't want an emergency situation or a kid-born-in-the-boondocks experience. The Asia-Pacific regional director had invited them to stay at his home until the baby arrived. "Two weeks would give us ample time," Colleen says.

Bob felt the trip to the island would take just a day, even if he only had an hour to visit the family. He decided to take their three-year-old son, Robby, with him so Colleen could finish preparing for the trip to the city.

Early the next morning, Bob with his small lad headed out the door for the boat dock. Just half an hour after saying good-bye to her "men," Colleen began to have gnawing thoughts of denial. Surely the twinges of pain that were coming and going were . . . No, they couldn't be. It was still 14 days away.

As the minutes ticked away with agonizing slowness, she realized that this was the day their awaited little one would probably arrive—not a couple of weeks later. All alone, the mixture of disbelief, fear, and excitement launched her into an audible prayer time. "O God, I need another miracle! Please, Father, help me know what to do if Bob doesn't make it home in time."

Thoughts raced through her head, none of them bringing her comfort. She had no way to contact Bob. The town had a public hospital, but it was overcrowded and had poor health standards. Animals roamed freely in the hallways where many patients lay due to lack of space. Proper refrigeration needed for lab work was impossible due to the daily, lengthy, nationwide brownouts, and there was no backup generator. In addition, the medical personnel had never heard of the Rh-negative blood factor, which she carried, and knew nothing about the necessary precautions should the newborn have positive blood. Only one pharmaceutical company in the country, located in Manila, had the capacity of special ordering the injections for the Rh factor. And at a great price! They had already made arrangements for Bob to pick up the ice-packed vials after the baby was born.

As Colleen scurried about the house, packing suitcases and making final preparations, she wondered, *Should I try to catch the public bus to Manila?* But there was no bus station, no set schedule. One just stood by the road and waited.

To further complicate matters, a typhoon was brewing and a heavy downpour had already started. Visions of a tall, blond lady, heavy with child in labor, drenched to the bone, waiting with her bags beside the road, brought comic relief to her in the day's confusion. "I remembered our landlady saying she had desires to be a midwife," Colleen says, "but had failed the course. I just had to laugh, wondering if I should give her an opportunity to practice."

In the meantime, Bob was blissfully unaware of the crisis at home. After two breakdowns on the island, he and Robby caught the last boat in the afternoon. They trudged in their front door at seven o'-clock, filthy from the trip.

"We need to go to Manila—*right now!*" Colleen announced, her voice giving extra emphasis to the last two words. Bob got the message.

Dirt and all, he promptly loaded the truck, and the trio sped away. They encountered many accidents due to the deluge. Only a miracle—maybe dozens of miracles—kept them safe as they avoided vehicles and people and creatures. And they made it to Manila in record time.

Going straight to the mission director's home to drop off Robby, the director offered to deliver the baby at his house, as he said he had experience in Vietnam. "Oh, no you won't!" Colleen objected. "I will not be one of your deputation stories!"

When Bob pulled into the hospital, which was guarded by security, he was informed that "reams" of paperwork must be completed before admittance, the urgency of the situation not clearly understood. But the frantic, father-to-be put Colleen in a wheelchair and barreled right in. Although the delivery room was off-limits to men, Bob didn't care. He was there and planned to stay. A staff member handed him scrubs to put on, but this brawny former football player burst them out at the seams.

Finally, the ER staff realized a baby was about to be born, and panic ensued. Can an intern deliver a baby? Certainly. Michael was delivered just fine and sent to a packed nursery that had rock music blasting away. There was no mistaking this light-complexioned baby!

The new mother had only a limited amount of time to spend with her newborn. "I was struck with the difference between Michael and Robby's births," Colleen says. "Our oldest son was born in Kansas City in a modern birthing room where the whole family could be with the baby. And the last night there, we had a steak dinner by candlelight. But in Manila, I only saw my baby for 30 minutes a day. For meals I ate rice and fish heads.

"But Michael was born safely. I'm just grateful I did not deliver him in our home or on a bus or . . . who knows where."

5
New Venue, New Challenges

You're being reassigned to Ukraine, probably living in Kyiv, the mission leaders had said.

Bob and Colleen sat surprised. *Stunned* might be a more appropriate word. They had just started a year of furlough when they learned of this unexpected and startling turn of events.

They had fully anticipated returning to the Philippines, where they had served for the past four years. They loved this Pacific Island nation and its people. This is where Colleen had grown up. The Filipinos were her people. This was "home."

Bob had adjusted well to the country and culture. He had learned Tagalog, the major language of the Filipinos, and even used this new language for preaching. He was content in the Philippines and felt fulfilled in his calling to missions.

Why? Why this move now? the Skinners wondered. The culture would be different. Literally everything would be different. Language. Climate. Customs. Food. Dress. Housing. Even the church. In the Philippines the church started mission work in 1946, right after World War II. But in Ukraine the church was new, only opened in 1992 after the iron curtain suddenly collapsed from around the Communist bloc.

We need experienced, career missionaries in Ukraine, and we trust God will lead you to accept, the Skinners had been told.

"Ukraine was the last place I ever thought I would end up," Colleen says. "But Bob and I agreed to pray about the matter." And they did. They prayed . . . considered . . . prayed . . . discussed . . . prayed . . . studied . . . prayed. When the Lord finally gave them peace about this new chapter in their lives, they informed the World Mission Department they would accept the assignment.

Their furlough was a year of preparation along with deputation. This major move required mental and emotional adjustment. "I knew very, very little about Ukraine," Colleen admits, "so I began to investigate. And what I learned fascinated me."

❋　❋　❋

Ukraine is inhabited by Slavic people who have been there since ancient times. They believed in pagan gods until Christianity was introduced; however, acceptance of Christian beliefs was only on the surface. The people still wanted to cling to their superstitions. Their true beliefs were rooted in animism, ancestral worship, and witchcraft. Each Slavic tribe had a totem animal, much like some Native Americans, and the worship of earth objects was common.

According to legend, Kiev is where the apostle Andrew came as a missionary.

The history of both Russia and Ukraine began with the establishment of a state at Kiev, also called

A church and monastery in Kyiv

Kievan Rus, in the A.D. 800s. The city of Kiev (now spelled Kyiv) was an important trading center on the Dnieper River, and this area became the first state of Russia.[1] One of the rulers, Vladimir the Great, accepted Christianity and made it the national religion in A.D. 988.

According to legend, Kiev is where the apostle Andrew came as a missionary. He raised a cross in Kiev and supposedly predicted that a great city would one day rise there with many churches to the glory of God. Through the centuries, Kiev slowly grew to become a great royal city with magnificent churches and cathedrals.

Poland conquered the western part of the country during the 1400s. During this time the region became known as Ukraine, meaning "frontier." Many men from Ukraine did not want to be ruled by the Poles, so they formed a group of soldier-outlaws called Cossacks. Even though the Cossacks became the defenders of the Christian faith, they were unable to defeat Poland. For the next 300 years, Poland, Russia, and Turkey fought for control of Ukraine. In spite of strong, ongoing Ukrainian opposition, the area came under Russian rule in the 1700s.[2]

When the Russian Revolution began in February 1917, Bolshevik troops invaded Ukraine 10 months later. Until the Union of Soviet Socialist Republics (USSR) was formed in 1922, swallowing Ukraine, the Bolsheviks and Ukrainians battled and the government changed hands many times.

As Stalin's grip on the USSR became tighter and tighter, he demanded more and more from the Ukrainians who lived in the "bread basket of Europe." In 1932-33, he created a man-made famine by taking every bit of food from the peasants. As a result, it is estimated 7 to 10 million starved to death. The decade of the 1930s became known as the Great Terror, as the Stalin government terrorized the Ukrainians even more with arrests, trials, exiles, and murders. He enforced strict censorship and banned religious life, destroying churches and dissolving Ukrainian institutions of education, science, and culture.[3]

During World War II, Hitler's armies invaded Ukraine. At first the people welcomed the Nazi troops, since they thought they would be freed from Stalin's power. But soon the Ukrainians awakened to the shocking reality that Hitler was there to steal their food and annex their land to Germany. In village after village, the invading soldiers burned every home and building, leaving the people homeless and

Bob and his sons visiting a farm in western Ukraine

starving. Protesters were executed on the spot. Needing workers for his depleted labor force, Hitler "kidnapped" Ukrainians—some estimate as many as 3 million—and took them to Germany. Treated as less than human, they became slaves for their Nazi master.[4] More than 5 million Ukrainians lost their lives during the war. And when the Soviet troops reoccupied Ukraine in 1944, a renewed wave of mass arrests, executions, and deportations swept through the country. Ukraine finally received its independence in 1991 with the breakup of the USSR.

The worst nuclear power plant disaster in the history of the world occurred in Chernobyl in 1986. Thousands upon thousands were killed or disabled, only adding to the Ukrainians' grief and misfortune.

Today, Kyiv is a major industrial, transportation, and cultural center with many parks and historical sites. The remains of ancient castles sit on the banks of the Dnieper River. The city is a foremost religious center. The cathedral of Saint Sophia is world renown for its frescoes and mosaics. Kyiv also boasts of a large university, a music conservatory, art museums, and one of Europe's largest sports stadiums.

Taras Shevchenko was a 19th-century author, poet, and painter. Born into a family of farmers, he became a symbol of Ukrainian spirit as he attacked Russian political, economic, and spiritual slavery in his writings. Shevchenko is honored with worldwide monuments, including one in Washington, D.C.

Although the people of Ukraine are, in general, poor and often face shortages of goods, yet much is produced in the country. It is one of the world's centers of sugar beet production. Other agricultural products include grain and vegetables. Natural resources have resulted in industrial growth with factories producing planes, ships, buses, computers, electronic equipment, chemicals, and textiles.

When the country was under Communist rule, the people had a sense of security. The government provided food, housing, education, and jobs. Although the people were poor, they were cared for. But when Communism broke down, all that the country provided its citizens disappeared. Suddenly, those who worked for the state had no salaries. Food lines became a reality. Shortages were widespread. When the people's utopia crumbled, they wondered how they would survive. The Ukrainians became a people without hope. Despair created massive societal problems—the escalation of broken homes, rising crime rate, increased alcoholism and drug abuse. In fact, public drunkenness became commonplace.

Into this climate of hopelessness, the Church of the Nazarene entered, bringing a life-changing, life-fulfilling message of full salvation.

✽ ✽ ✽

"I was apprehensive about going to a communist country," Colleen admits, "yet I knew the Lord would take care of us." Upon arriving in Ukraine in

The Skinners at Odessa, Ukraine, on the Black Sea, 1995

1995, Colleen and Bob found themselves transplanted into a mixture of old world and modern surroundings. This intriguing country, after a troubled past, years of tyranny, and seven decades of Communist rule, seemed to be open for Christianity. The Church of the Nazarene had officially entered four years before, and two short-term missionary couples who preceded them had sowed precious seed in Ukrainian soil.

The Skinners' assignment as the first career missionaries in Ukraine was to direct the work of the church, including the services and resources of compassionate ministries. In Kyiv they found the small group of Nazarenes meeting in a rented auditorium, being forced to move the location of their worship services several times in their brief history. The church rented adjacent rooms for Sunday School and office space. But this latest facility presented many challenges: the auditorium and rooms had no heat, no telephone, and often no electricity; property management could rent out the auditorium on Sundays without notice; and the rent continued to rise.

"On a couple of occasions," Colleen says, "the police showed up during our church staff meetings and interrogated us, accusing us of not paying the rent. But upon further investigation we learned the building manager had been pocketing the money.

"We knew the task would be immense, but fortunately, at that time, we didn't know how immense. We just felt God was using all these hardships and problems to somehow help us obtain our own place for worship and ministry."

By law the Church of the Nazarene could not buy land in Kyiv and construct its own facility, and any building they purchased could not be demolished and rebuilt. Bob quickly found out that even old, deteriorated buildings were selling for a premium, and the church would encounter much red tape in every part of the process.

"This was an opportunity for growth in grace, faith, and holiness," Colleen says. "But our God provided a building that we could remodel into a ministry center, and He supplied the means every step of the way. And we were blessed beyond our greatest hopes with several skilled and dedicated Work and Witness teams. Each one was special in the way they embraced the people and ministered among them. All team members let the light of Christ shine brightly from their lives as they worked hard and made sacrifices to help us with our new building."

With much rejoicing the small Nazarene congregation finally moved the worship services and weekly ministries to their own site. It truly became a ministry center, though far from finished. The church people were able to watch the progress and see God answering prayer.

Often the pianist had to play with gloves on, and the people could see their breath as they sang.

During the warmer months, the group met outside in a tent, moving inside as the weather demanded. Heat was still unavailable for the long, cold months. But those steadfast believers just bundled up from head to toe and did not forsake assembling together, faithfully gathering week after week to praise God and spur each other on to love and good deeds. Often the pianist had to play with gloves on, and the people could see their breath as they sang. "But God's presence was so real and precious," Colleen says.

Sundays looked similar to any other Sabbath service in the denomination. It began with Sunday School for the children, a teen program, and Bible study for adults. Worship had a familiar look but not sound; the language was Ukrainian. In the sanctuary there was a screen and projector for the words to choruses, a sound system, and chairs with songbooks on them. The congregational singing included joyful and enthusiastic accompaniment on keyboard, guitar, violin, and flute. The order of service would make any Nazarene feel right at home. For the worshipers who lacked proficiency in Ukrainian, there was English interpretation.

One observation Bob and Colleen have made, however, is that the style of worship seems to be a more important topic in the United States than in Ukraine. In Ukraine the worship is a combination of contemporary and traditional Greek Orthodox. "Music is not the controversial issue that it is in America," Colleen says. "Also Ukrainians would be surprised that Communion is not celebrated as much in the States as it is in their country. To the Christians in Ukraine, Communion is the highest form of worship."

One section of the ministry center is devoted to

compassionate ministries, which has become a dynamic and successful method of reaching people for Christ. The Kyiv church started an outreach ministry to handicapped people who no longer received care after the Soviet government fell. Out of this ministry, a Bible study began. Later this excited group of believers—on their own—decided they wanted to become an official church. "It was such a deep joy to watch this young church grow and develop," Colleen says.

This fledgling congregation became involved in compassionate ministries themselves. When people in western Ukraine were devastated by flooding, the Kyiv church took hundreds of boxes of clothing, food, medicines, and Bibles to the victims.

Out of this outreach effort and others like it, God began opening doors for ministry in this area of Ukraine. "Medical Work and Witness teams have poured themselves out in long, hard hours of love, care, and sacrifice," Colleen says. "In situations of seemingly endless need, their witness had been strong and bright."

One area of inspiring growth has been among children and young people. The summer after the Skinners arrived, they conducted the first Nazarene Vacation Bible School (VBS) along with youth and children's camps. And each summer the number involved escalated, both the children and youth who attended and the adults who offered to serve in these ministries.

"One year some dear friends from Bob's home church decided to visit Ukraine and bring their own Work and Witness family team," Colleen remembers.

"The couple's three daughters helped with puppets and crafts and sports. These precious people helped sponsor the first camps on the eastern side of Ukraine.

"Then a tremendous team of young people from the Philadelphia District came and did a fantastic job at the camps in Kyiv. They slept in cabins with the young campers and ate in the dining hall. I remember one team member commenting, 'I can't believe it! I came all the way to Ukraine to eat camp food!' It was a marvelous experience for both groups, the Ukrainians and Americans."

During the camps, Colleen played her guitar at campfire events. She willingly took time to talk with the kids, even serving as interpreter. They laughed a lot about situations they encountered. And the Lord blessed her and Bob's efforts. "That summer was the beginning of a complete turnaround for the youth program," Colleen says. "From that time on, the weekly Bible study and Sunday School grew in numbers and spiritual depth. The young people became involved in service projects, particularly to orphans, and truly learned to give of themselves."

❊   ❊   ❊

Time approached for the district assembly—the fifth official assembly for the Ukraine District. General Superintendent Jerry Porter and his wife, Toni, were coming, and everyone was excited.

"In planning for this event," Colleen says, "Bob and I, along with our people, had a chance to reflect on all we had been privileged to see that God had done in the past three and half years. We knew when the church assigned us to Ukraine that we were coming to a small group of discouraged yet faithful new Christians. It was a thrill to watch those precious folks deepening their faith and walk with God and, in turn, pouring out themselves in ministry."

One thing that blessed Colleen and Bob was seeing people hunger to grow and learn. "It was so much fun to teach missions classes, because the people were eager to absorb everything," Colleen says. "They earnestly took notes, read everything they were given in Russian on the subject, and tackled class projects with zeal. And they were like this with every class that was offered."

Many took classes for credit through European Nazarene Bible College (now European Nazarene College), and two students even went to Nazarene Theological Seminary in Kansas City for a summer intensive session toward a master's program.

Educational opportunities were taken to eastern Ukraine, where the Lord opened doors for four new congregations. Since it took 24 hours by train to reach three of those locations, plus the pastors did not have telephones, this created a challenge to help them feel part of the larger church body.

"How exciting that each of them were to be represented at the district assembly," Colleen says. "And what an opportunity to provide them a bigger picture of what God was doing as well as a reminder they were not alone out there. We want Nazarenes to take note that the church in Ukraine is alive and well!"

Notes

1. *The World Book Encyclopedia*, s.v. "Ukraine."
2. *The World Book Encyclopedia*.
3. "Chronology of Key Historic Events"
<www.ukraine.online.com.ua/UKR_ENG/chron/en.htm>
4. Olga Kaczmar, "The Sad History of the 'Two' Ukraines."
<http://home.earthlink.net/~okaczmar/histukr.html>

6
Some Difference-Makers

Bob was trying to set up his office in the newly purchased building. The floors needed work, the walls begged for a new paint job, and the entire structure cried out for a thorough cleaning. Sergei and Lesya were there to lend a hand.

Sergei had been a professional guitarist in a rock band. The Skinners befriended him and Lesya, inviting them to tea and then to church. The couple started attending with their two children and never stopped coming. God delivered Sergei from tobacco, and he and Lesya became excited, contagious Christians.

Sergei accepted the ministry of *JESUS* film coordinator and began showing it in some of the outlying towns. In many villages he discovered people in desperate need of medical attention as a result of the nuclear accident at Chernobyl. He recruited doctors from Kyiv First Church to treat adults, youth, and children with thyroid and other problems. After people waited for medical care during the day, they waited again, sometimes for hours, for the evening service. Sergei was there, waiting with them, singing and playing his guitar.

"Sergei and Lesya's greatest desire is for their

children to grow up to serve the Lord," Colleen says. "They are making a difference for the Lord. And, by the way, with their willing hands and hearts, the ministry center was painted and cleaned."

❋   ❋   ❋

Andre, a precocious young man, had a intense interest in electronics. Somehow he located parts and built a radio receiver, which was strictly illegal in Russia. Turning the dial, he found a broadcast sponsored by the Church of the Nazarene. Intrigued, he listened yet knowing it was dangerous to do so. Twice he tuned in. Later, the authorities caught him with the radio and sent him to prison. While there he foraged for parts again and built another radio.

Meanwhile, a friend of Andre was handed a tract about Kyiv First Church while riding a train. As he read it, he knew that Andre, recently released from prison, would be interested. He found the newly freed friend in Mariupol and gave him the tract.

Eagerly, Andre wrote to the church. One day Bob spotted the letter in a huge stack of unanswered mail on his desk and sent a reply to Andre, inviting him to come to Kyiv. And the curious, inquiring young man did. He stayed, learned about the church, committed his life to Christ, attended Bible studies, and took additional classes. Today, Andre is back in his hometown of Mariupol, where he planted a church and is serving as the pastor. What a difference-maker!

*　*　*

Walter Cisco, a widower who donated a large sum of money for the ministry center, flew to Ukraine from the States for the dedication. With him were some family members and friends, among them a special lady friend. For some reason, Ukrainian food and Walter did not get along, and he became quite sick. His family and friends tried to make him comfortable, and while he rested, they went sightseeing.

Vera, a good and generous Russian lady, loved to take care of people. She knew about Walter's illness, so she did what any "good and generous" Russian woman would do: she brought him some borscht and nursed him. When Walter got better, he and those with him were invited to a church member's house for dinner. Vera was invited too and just happened to find herself seated between Walter and his special lady.

Walter and Vera had a pleasant time talking that evening. And when he returned home, the talking continued. In fact, he made four trips back to Kyiv. Over time he and Vera fell in love. She traveled to the United States, and the two were married.

In America Vera experienced culture shock. She moved from a small one-room apartment in Ukraine to a large home with many rooms. "It took a long time for her to figure out everything in the kitchen," Colleen says. "All those gadgets were a total mystery to her."

Today, Vera and Walter's mission is helping raise

money in the United States for church buildings in Ukraine. They truly are difference-makers.

* * *

Oksana grew up in an atheist home. As a young person, she went to a Soviet camp to become a Communist Young Pioneer. Decorated with Communist flags, symbols, and signs, the camp's purpose was to indoctrinate the youth.

Oksana was introduced to the Church of the Nazarene in her early 20s by a friend. Already engaged to an atheist, Oksana and her fiancé married. But Oksana felt drawn to the church and kept attending. The Holy Spirit spoke to her softly, gently urging her to choose eternal life found only in Jesus. Oksana responded and became a new creation in Christ.

Her husband, however, refused to attend church. Oksana was the lone light in her family, and ultimately all of the problems the couple encountered were blamed on her and her "religion."

Determined and happy in the Lord, Oksana persevered. Because she had an incredible way with children, she accepted a Sunday School class. She loved this assignment and handled it with passion and zeal. "I took our children to Oksana's class," Colleen says, "because I could see how good she was with children."

Oksana is a teacher, but she received no pay from teaching in the state school. "I had been praying for a tutor for our boys," Colleen says, "so I asked Oksana if she would do it—for pay, of course. And she agreed. She tutored the boys for two to three hours a day, five days a week. And in the process, all our family learned Russian."

As Oksana became better acquainted with the neighborhood Sunday School kids, they loved her, and she loved them. The church asked her to direct VBS and the children's camp, and she became the children's director for the Ukraine District. Later she traveled to Moscow to enroll in Bible courses and then returned to Kyiv to teach the same subjects.

"Oksana is an outstanding servant of God, a genuine difference-maker," Colleen states. "She holds a special place in our hearts and church. And we are still praying for her husband to accept Christ."

✻   ✻   ✻

Bob and Colleen have a burden for the elderly people of Ukraine. Since the overthrow of Communism, senior citizens have found life difficult. The government no longer cares for them, and they have no means of income. Most find it hard to get to the store for food and basic supplies. Many suffer from the winter's cold due to the lack of heat. And if heat is available, funds are inadequate to pay for it.

In the apartment building where the Skinners live, many elderly people reside on the upper floors. These people took occupancy during the Communist rule, receiving their

"Sometimes Bob has literally picked up one of these dear folks," Colleen says, "and carried them up the long flight of stairs."

The Skinners sharing a meal with a Ukrainian family

apartments for life. As the residents age, they find it more and more difficult to climb the stairs to their homes. Elevators are nonexistent. "Sometimes Bob has literally picked up one of these dear folks," Colleen says, "and carried them up the long flight of stairs."

One older lady in Kyiv First Church suffered from Parkinson's disease. Paying for the medication was impossible for her. "Since Bob knew a pharmacist," Colleen says, "he prevailed upon his friend to provide the expensive medicine for this dear lady. She was profoundly grateful but had no way to say thank you. Then little trinkets began to appear in Bob's office. She was parting with treasured items from her home to express her gratitude."

❋ ❋ ❋

"Although the Ukrainians live hard lives," Colleen says, "when they are reached with the gospel, they become joyful, enthusiastic, dedicated Christians. Learning to serve the Lord is no problem for them, because there is such a great need all around them. We are so grateful for people, such as Sergei and Lesya, Andre, and Oksana. They are examples of what God's grace and heart holiness can do to transform people into Kingdom disciples. But leadership development is an urgent need. We ask that people pray for God to raise up workers for the harvest and call Ukrainians into full-time ministry—to be authentic difference-makers."

7

Happy, Hectic Family

Settling in Kyiv became the number one priority in the summer of 1995. While Bob was busy with mission responsibilities, Colleen was home with two young boys, setting up housekeeping. Although the church had given them a warm reception, Colleen desired to get to know her neighbors. "I would say hello to them when I was out," she says, "and they would turn and walk away. And this went on for the first six months."

The children in the neighborhood refused to play with Robby and Michael, often being "quite mean" to them. Colleen was in tears night after night.

Then their first Christmas in Kyiv approached. This holiday is one the Ukrainians do not celebrate, or at least emphasize, because they had no religion as such for decades.

That December Bob had taken a group of teens to the Netherlands, and Colleen was home alone with the boys. She decided to make Christmas cookies. "We baked and decorated and baked and decorated," she says. "We broke some of them and even sampled several small pieces. All in all the cookies were a sad-looking affair."

Colleen and her little elves arranged them on red plates, covered them with plastic wrap, and attached a Russian Bible verse on top. Then they went door-to-door in their apartment building to give away their treats.

First they traipsed downstairs to visit an older couple. When Colleen knocked on their door, the man growled in Russian, "Who's there?" Colleen tried to explain in her broken Russian who they were and why they were there. Finally the man cracked the door, obviously angry at the intrusion from these "foreigners."

There stood Michael, a darling cherub, in front of his mother and brother with a plate of cookies. Colleen nudged her son forward, and the codger opened the door. Michael handed the gift to the unsmiling man, then quickly hid behind his mother. "Our neighbor was noticeably surprised," Colleen says. "Instead of yelling at us, as we expected, he took the cookies and thanked us profusely. Later that day he came upstairs with the plate and returned it with four pieces of candy.

"That changed everything," Colleen continues. "Word got around, and the people opened up and became our friends. That first Christmas it didn't take very long to deliver the cookies to our neighbors. But by the second Christmas, it took two hours to deliver just two plates of treats because we were warmly welcomed into their homes to visit."

❊   ❊   ❊

The Skinners live on the third floor of a five-story apartment building. "We have the *best* home in Kyiv!" says Michael. The Skinner residence has three rooms, where most apartments have only one room.

"Though this may not be the best neighborhood," Colleen says, "it's quite nice. The living room is small with a couch, chairs, tables, and TV. The kitchen has a stove, sink, and refrigerator with pictures held on by magnets. It really looks like a typical home in the States."

Colleen cooks the traditional Ukrainian dish called borscht.* "This is the most popular food in Ukraine," she says, "and it was first cooked here. Although other cultures have adopted this 'delicacy,' it originated in Ukraine." Borscht is a mildly tart, thick soup whose main ingredient is beets and may contain as many as 20 items. Recipes with different combinations and proportions vary from family to family. While some people say true Ukrainian borscht has beans, that fact is up for debate.

"Borscht is usually made from a base of rich meat stock, often pork, as pork is more readily available than beef," Colleen adds. "Meatless versions are served on days of fasting and when meat is not available. The tart flavor comes from one or more of the following: fermented beet juice, lemon juice, strained rhubarb juice, vinegar, or pickle brine. Borscht also tastes of salt, pepper, dill, and garlic. It has a deep red color and should not be mushy. And just before serving, a dollop of sour cream is added. In fact, sour

---

*Colleen's recipe for borscht is located on page 85.

cream is served with almost everything, and garlic is used liberally."

On a typical day, the boys eat breakfast of eggs or pancakes. A wide variety of cereals packaged in colorful boxes do not exist, but sometimes they have "foreign" corn flakes. Then the boys head out to a public school. Classes are held in both Russian and Ukrainian. "And it is really hard," the boys declare.

While the kids are in school, Colleen goes grocery shopping, which takes longer than in the States. Supermarkets? None. Instead there are different shops for every-thing. "At an open market, I can buy potatoes, vegetables, and meat," Colleen says. "But the meat—which is quite expensive—is not butchered. I just point out what I want, and it's cut on the spot. Ground meat is not available, so it's ground at home. Often there are shortages of different items, so I must check the newspaper to keep up with what is available. I buy bread at a bakery, which is an old Soviet store, but I can only get it at certain times. When we first arrived, it took us awhile to figure out the system, and I admit, until we did, we experienced a few hunger pangs."

Receiving a LINKS box is an exciting event. And the Skinners use everything. They love to get items the Ukrainians have never seen—especially peanut butter. Colleen made some peanut butter

> The kids looked at this strange food, smelled it, and cautiously took a bite. Surprise! They gobbled it down.

sandwiches with this treat from a LINKS package and offered this kid-favorite snack to the neighborhood children for a picnic. The kids looked at this strange food, smelled it, and cautiously took a bite. Surprise! They gobbled it down. Colleen began to get knocks on the door from these little ones, asking, "Picnic? Picnic?"

"Jell-O is also a novelty, and the children just love it," Colleen says. "We always welcome baking ingredients, such as brown sugar, cream of tartar, and shortening, which are hard to find. And we are delighted to receive tea bags and hot cocoa mix."

The most valued boxes contain medical supplies and equipment, such as bandages, syringes, and medical books. "And we value the containers of clothing," Colleen says. "We take the used garments out to small villages and distribute them. It's become an important way to gain the trust of the people who still need to hear the gospel."

❊ ❊ ❊

Bob is busy—all day, every day. He's up early and goes until 10 or 11 at night. "There is so much to do," Colleen says. "The ministry center here in Ukraine is a full-time job itself. Seeing to the needs of people takes a lot of his time. In addition, he's involved in ministry across all of Ukraine, and he travels throughout Europe. He's a wonderful speaker and storyteller with a tremendous sense of humor. Warmhearted and personable, Bob is loved by people everywhere. But he has another side to him as well: he's a great family man. One time when I was away, he surprised me by remodeling our kitchen. He loves our kids and has had a large part in caring for them, even as babies. He could change diapers with the best of dads."

Colleen is a huge asset to Bob in the ministry. This busy missionary wife and mom leads the worship team, which requires practice time as well. Other responsibilities include assisting in the office; helping with children's ministry, weekly Bible studies, and a ladies' missionary group; entertaining; teaching courses; and conducting neighborhood outreach. One wonders when she has time to sleep. But in talking about her life as a missionary, she says, "I just love what we're doing in Ukraine. It's fun to help people."

> I just love what we're doing in Ukraine. It's fun to help people.

Kyiv First Church's building is now complete, thanks to many Work and Witness teams. "But several churches still lack buildings," Colleen says. "There are lots of Work and Witness projects here. And if an entire team is not available, volunteers can come to Ukraine and help on their own. There's always plenty to do."

One group of ladies from a Work and Witness team stayed in an apartment in the Skinners' building. The women cooked for themselves and came across a Teflon pan they felt needed attention, since the coating was coming off in ribbons. They scrubbed and scrubbed until all the Teflon was gone and shiny as new. When the apartment owner re-

The Skinners on furlough

turned and saw the pan, she was perplexed. Showing the utensil to Colleen, she said, "Don't they have Teflon in America?"

❉ ❉ ❉

Furlough is a hectic time for the Skinners, as it is for any missionary family. While on home assignment, Bob and Colleen live near their kids' grandparents, a practice Colleen remembers from her own childhood. Only now they stay in Idaho near her father. "One of the joys of living in Idaho is having lots of relatives around," Colleen continues. "The boys have kids to play with, and they really like their cousins, aunts, and uncles." Since Bob's parents are not too far away in Oregon, they often keep the three boys while Bob and sometimes Colleen travel.

"Deputation can be brutal," Colleen says. "Bob's speaking schedule is quite demanding. One year he preached in 200 churches alone. After that furlough he was ready to go back to the mission field to get some rest. Being a people person, he enjoys speaking and visiting very much, but deputation takes him away from the kids. So we have arranged for the boys to take turns going with him, and that way each receives some 'dad time.'"

One time Bob was scheduled to speak at a church in Idaho near their furlough home. Colleen was excited and told the kids they were going to travel there and see Daddy.

"Who?" asked baby Joshua.

"Daddy," Colleen responded. "We're going to see Daddy!"

"Oh," the little tyke said. "You mean Uncle Bob."

After one furlough, Robby was experiencing a hard time readjusting to life in Kyiv. He missed his grandparents and family back in the States. As Bob was preparing to leave on a ministry trip one night, Robby sighed and asked his mom, "Can't we just retire?"

Such is the life of missionaries who in obedience to God travel to "the far side of the sea" to serve Him.

The Legacy Goes On

The Skinner's children are the treasures of their parents' hearts. Bob has often referred to his boys as "cherubs." As they are growing older, their cherubic characteristics are slowly disappearing. Yet, they are happy, well-adjusted children who are loved and cherished.

Robby, now 12, is tall, handsome, and serious. He loves to collect coins. On one furlough he was invited to a classmate's birthday party. He bought a present, and his mother drove him there on the appointed day. As they pulled up in front of the house, the lad became agitated. He studied the house, saying, "This can't be right! This house is a mansion!" Robby was not used to seeing one huge house for just one family. He thought lots of families must be living there. When he was reluctant to go in, Colleen walked him to the door.

"How do we deal with differences in lifestyle?" Colleen asks rhetorically. "When in the United States, we limit trips to the mall and Toys R Us, because it's too overwhelming."

Michael, age 9, is a strawberry blonde who tells Ukrainians that he's a Filipino. He speaks Russian fast and furiously. One day he dashed into their

The "cherubs": Robby, Michael, and Joshua

apartment and told his mother, "We need some cool-looking bottles. We're playing bar."

"How do we get across to a child," Colleen says, "that being drunk all the time is not acceptable when that is what they see so much of?"

Joshua is an adorable, easygoing 5-year-old with no fear of adventure. On the last furlough, his parents dropped him off with grandparents he had never seen. Yet he was quite content to stay with these "strangers."

* * *

"I realize that I have a great heritage," Colleen says. "My earliest memories started in our home in the Philippines where my siblings and I were part of missions. My family went out into the world, to *the far side of the sea*, to invite people to come to Christ. I can't underestimate the tremendous influence that being part of building the Church of the Nazarene has had on my life. This is the church where I knelt to receive Jesus. And my parents taught me that discipleship was important and modeled it their whole lives."

> I fervently pray that the passion passed on to me by my parents will be implanted in our precious children.

Colleen feels she has to carry this legacy on. Her own kids are part of the same process she was growing up. "Our boys participate when we invite neighborhood people in and when Work and Witness teams come. Our sons are in the thick of it too. And they sometimes go with their father to other parts of Ukraine to minister with him. They are part of the whole church family."

What does Colleen want to pass on to Robby, Michael, and Joshua? "I want them to understand what true wealth is," she says, "that it's not in 'things' so abundant in the United States. Rather, riches come by giving away—giving to people who have nothing. I see our sons growing up, going away to school, being a part of mission activities, obtaining a bigger picture of the world, and possessing a greater love for God. I hope they will not become consumed with themselves but will be unselfish and giving Christians. I fervently pray that the passion passed on to me by my parents will be implanted in our precious children."

82

Colleen was a missionary's child by chance. She became a missionary by choice. And now she is giving that chance for choice to her own children.

And the legacy goes on.

Appendix
Borscht Recipe

10 cups beef stock
2 cups beets, shredded, or 2 cans diced beets, undrained
1 onion, chopped
2 carrots, diced
½ cup celery, diced
2 potatoes, diced
½ cup green beans or white northern beans, undrained
2 cups cabbage, shredded
1 cup tomato juice
2 garlic cloves, minced
1 tbsp. flour
2 tbsp. lemon juice
1 tbsp. dill, cut up finely
1 cup sour cream
1 lb. pork or stew beef (optional)

If meat is used, cut in small chunks and simmer in stock until tender. (Note: borscht is often cooked without meat.) Add all of the ingredients except the beets, and cook until vegetables are soft. Add beets and cook for an additional 10-15 minutes. Serve hot, or refrigerate to serve cold later. Top each serving with a dollop of sour cream. Makes 10-12 servings.

Pronunciation Guide

Andre	ahn-DRAY
Batangas	bah-TAHN-gahs
Bolsheviks	BOHL-shuh-vihks
borscht	BOHRSH(T)
Chernobyl	chair-NOH-buhl
Cossacks	KAH-suhks
Dnieper	NEE-per
Kievan Rus	KEE-uh-fuhn ROOS
Kyiv	KEE-ehf
Lesya	LAY-see-uh
Mariupol	mahr-ee-OO-puhl
Oksana	ohk-SAH-nuh
Sergei	sehr-GAY
Shevchenko, Taras	shehf-CHEHNG-koh TAHR-uhs
Ukraine	yoo-KRAYN
Vladimir	VLAD-uh-mihr